A SPECIAL BOOK ABOUT ME

D1509118

'There's a kid at school who gets extra help from a special teacher. He has temper tantrums when he is angry and sometimes finds it hard to pay attention. He might even have been to a special school to learn how to behave appropriately in class. One day this kid started to ask questions like, "Why do I feel different – am I not like other kids?" This kid might be a little different from others in some ways...but this kid is NOT STUPID! Can you solve the mystery of the special kid?'

This book offers a fun and accessible introduction for a child diagnosed with Asperger Syndrome (AS).

Intended as a support tool in the initial period after diagnosis, *A Special Book About Me* is varied and engaging, and addresses questions or concerns that the child might have, such as 'What are the characteristics of AS?', 'Why did it happen to me?', and 'What happens now?'.

Also included are poems, stories, illustrations and activities to help them come to terms with and move forward from a diagnosis of AS.

A Special Book About Me is essential reading for children in the initial period after a diagnosis of AS.

Josie Santomauro is a full-time writer living in Brisbane, Australia. Her son, Damian, was diagnosed with AS at the age of five. She has written numerous fiction books for children and young adults, and several books on AS. She regularly gives seminars and talks on AS.

Jessica Kingsley *Publishers*
116 Pentonville Road
London N1 9JB, UK

400 Market Street, Suite 400
Philadelphia, PA 19106, USA

www.jkp.com

Cover design: del norte (Leeds) Ltd

Books in the same series

You Are Special Too
A Book for Brothers and Sisters of Children Diagnosed with Asperger Syndrome
Josie Santomauro
Illustrated by Carla Marino
ISBN 978 1 84310 656 2
Asperger Syndrome: After the Diagnosis series

Mothering Your Special Child
A Book for Mothers or Carers of Children Diagnosed with Asperger Syndrome
Josie Santomauro
Illustrated by Carla Marino
ISBN 978 1 84310 657 9
Asperger Syndrome: After the Diagnosis series

Fathering Your Special Child
A Book for Fathers or Carers of Children Diagnosed with Asperger Syndrome
Josie Santomauro
Illustrated by Carla Marino
ISBN 978 1 84310 658 6
Asperger Syndrome: After the Diagnosis series

Your Special Grandchild
A Book for Grandparents of Children Diagnosed with Asperger Syndrome
Josie Santomauro
Illustrated by Carla Marino
ISBN 978 1 84310 659 3
Asperger Syndrome: After the Diagnosis series

Your Special Student
A Book for Educators of Children Diagnosed with Asperger Syndrome
Josie Santomauro and Margaret-Anne Carter
Illustrated by Carla Marino
ISBN 978 1 84310 660 9
Asperger Syndrome: After the Diagnosis series

Your Special Friend
A Book for Peers of Children Diagnosed with Asperger Syndrome
Josie Santomauro
Illustrated by Carla Marino
ISBN 978 1 84310 661 6
Asperger Syndrome: After the Diagnosis series

A Special Book About Me

A Book for Children Diagnosed
with Asperger Syndrome

JOSIE SANTOMAURO

Illustrated by Carla Marino

Jessica Kingsley Publishers
London and Philadelphia

First published in 2009
by Jessica Kingsley Publishers
116 Pentonville Road
London N1 9JB, UK

and

400 Market Street, Suite 400
Philadelphia, PA 19106, USA

www.jkp.com

Library of Congress Cataloging in Publication Data
Santomauro, J. (Josie)
A special book about me : a book for children diagnosed with Asperger syndrome /
Josie Santomauro.
p. cm.
ISBN 978-1-84310-655-5 (pb : alk. paper) 1. Asperger's syndrome--Popular works.
I. Title.
RJ506.A9S366 2009
618.92'858832--dc22

2008041279

British Library Cataloguing in Publication Data
A CIP catalogue record for this book is available from the British Library

ISBN 978 1 84310 655 5

Printed and bound in Great Britain by
Athenaeum Press, Gateshead, Tyne and Wear

To Damian
My special son

Thank you to all the wonderful
contributors who have given
permission to reprint their gifts of
poetry, reflections, writings and
private thoughts here in this
book.

Contents

The Case

- There's a kid at school who gets help from a special teacher.

- Maybe they also visit a speech therapist.

- They may go to some sort of special classes to learn how to cope with teasing.

- This kid has even been to a special school to learn how to improve their behaviour in class.

One day this kid starts to ask questions:

- Why do I have to go to that special school, when other kids in my class don't?

- Why do I need a special teacher to help me?

- Why do I have to go to different types of doctors?

- Why do I feel different – I'm not like other kids?

This kid might be a little different from others in some ways…but this kid is *not stupid*!

Why do you think this kid needs all this help?

Let's dig up some clues and find out…

Four Clues Found

This kid needs extra help in four areas:

1. Social skills – practising being a friend

2. Communication – talking with people

3. Behaviour

4. Sensory stimulation.

When a person needs help so they can get on with everyday life, they may have a disability.

Look at these different types of help others need:

- a person who needs a wheelchair to move around

- a person who needs glasses to see

- a person who needs a puffer for asthma

- a person who needs to use a cane to walk

- a person who needs help to speak clearly

- a person who needs a hearing aid to hear.

Solve the Mystery

When you add up these four clues:

1. needs help with practising to be a friend
2. needs help with talking with people
3. needs help with improving their behaviour
4. needs help with sensory stimulation, as they can find bright lights or noise, for example, very stressful

they equal a disability called *Asperger Syndrome.*

Asperger Syndrome might make life seem a little hard for this kid

but

Asperger Syndrome also makes this kid extra special in some ways.

Do you think you know someone who has Asperger Syndrome?

Congratulations! You have solved the mystery of the special kid.

You are that special kid.

You have Asperger Syndrome.

Do you know anyone else who has Asperger Syndrome?

Write their names here:

. . . .

. . . .

. . . .

Mystery Word Identified

A nger and frustration

S tress and anxiety

P roblems with speech and language

E asily distracted

R eality/Fiction confusion

G ross motor skills

E ccentric or odd behaviours

R igid and doesn't like change

S ocial skills

Y ou are intelligent

N o eye contact

D on't like loud noises and crowds

R ote memory

O bsessional

M aking friends is hard

E mpathy

Let's Take a Closer Look at Asperger Syndrome

Anger and frustration

- I may have temper tantrums when I'm angry.
- I might find it hard to ask for help when I feel confused or frustrated.

Stress and anxiety

- I don't like to be teased.
- I can sometimes get anxious over changes.
- I can sometimes get stressed at school.
- I need help to learn how to relax and to keep calm.
- I need help to ignore teasing and bullying.

Problems with speech and language

- Sometimes I don't realize that my voice is too loud, or that is sounds 'different'.
- Sometimes I can't express what I am thinking or what I am feeling.
- Sometimes I can't understand what people are trying to tell me.

Easily distracted

- Sometimes my room and school desk is untidy.
- Sometimes I forget what someone said to me.
- Sometimes it's hard to pay attention, especially in a busy classroom.

Reality/Fiction confusion

- Sometimes I don't understand jokes or stories.
- I might sometimes believe my dreams are real.
- I can get confused if people say things like, 'Pull your socks up'.

Gross motor skills

- Sometimes I can be clumsy.
- I might find some sports (especially ball games) a little hard to play.

Eccentric or odd behaviours

- I may have different behaviours to other kids.
- Other kids may think I'm a bit weird.
- I might do everyday things differently to everyone else.

Rigid and doesn't like change

- I like it better when things don't change.
- I really like things to stay the same.
- I like to know what is going to happen next.

Social skills

- I might find it hard to understand people's body language, like if they're bored when I'm talking.
- I like to talk about my hobbies all the time.
- I may not understand social 'rules' and may sometimes seem rude.

You are intelligent

- I may be very intelligent – especially at maths, science and computers.
- Some doctors call me 'little professor'.
- I may go to university when I grow up.

No eye contact

- I don't like to look at people's eyes when I talk to them.

- I might look at the ground instead of their face, but I am still listening to them.

Don't like loud noises and crowds

- Loud noises can hurt my ears, and bright light may hurt my eyes.

- I don't like noisy or crowded places, like shopping centres or parties.

Rote memory

- I might remember things that happened a long time ago.
- I have a good memory for facts and figures.

Obsessional

- If I really like something I can talk on and on…and on…about it.
- Sometimes I do or say something over and over like flapping my hands, touching my face or repeating a word.

Making friends is hard

- I might not have a lot of friends.
- Maybe I'd like to have more friends.
- I might not be interested in friends.
- I sometimes find it hard to make friends.

Empathy

- Sometimes I can't understand how other people are feeling – like if they are happy or sad.

But here are some other features of Asperger Syndrome:

A rtistic

S mart

P unctual

E ngaging

R epetitive movements

G ood natured

E xtraordinary

R ules

S ignificant

Y why? Asks lots of questions

N atural

D etermined

R esourceful

O ver sensitive

M aths wiz

E motional

How Did Asperger Syndrome Happen?

- You didn't catch it like a cold or the chicken pox.

- It's not your fault or your parents' – it's nobody's fault!

- You could've been born with Asperger Syndrome.

- There is no special cure or magic potion to fix Asperger Syndrome.

- Doctors think a small part of your brain is working differently to other people's.

You're not the only one with Asperger Syndrome.

At least one in every 150 people in the world has Asperger Syndrome.

How to Learn More about Asperger Syndrome

Join the local Asperger Syndrome support group.

Chat on the internet with other kids with Asperger Syndrome (remember to ask your parents for help).

Attend classes that help with friendship and communication.

Talk with your doctor or therapist.

Talk to your parents or a family member.

Read books about Asperger Syndrome.

The Special Kids Assistants

Ask an adult to help you fill in this page.

Write down who, what, how and why people and things help you.

WHO?	WHAT?	HOW?	WHY?
Parents	*Make up charts*	*Using coloured pens and paper*	*To remind me and help me be independent*
Family			
Doctor			
Teacher			
Special teacher			
Government			
Therapist			
Friends			

I'm a Great Detective
Always on the Lookout

Just by learning to help myself, I can:

- lead a happy life

and

- be a successful citizen.

Time out

- Before you get too stressed at school or at home you can take yourself to time out.

- This can be an area of the classroom that you and your teacher have decided you can use. In this area you may have a beanbag to sit in, and a box with calm down items, e.g. stress ball.

Diary

- Look at your school diary every day so you know what is happening at school when you get there.

- Add the dates of any changes or new things that are going to happen into your diary.

- Write in birthdays, lessons, etc. into your diary so you don't forget them.

Remember

- Make a 'remembering book' – a tiny notebook with a small pencil.

- Keep it in your pocket at school for taking notes or remembering names, etc. Especially when visitors come to the classroom and you want to remember who they were and what they said.

Positive

- When you feel sad, you can think of things you like to do or things or people who make you happy, like your pet or a grandparent, a game or aunt/uncle who you like very much.

- You can try to laugh and have fun by remembering times that you have enjoyed, maybe a day out with your grandparents.

- You can read a joke book or make up your own jokes.

Journal

- You can keep a journal at home and write your thoughts and feelings in it.

- You can try to write in it every day whether you feel happy or sad. It is a good place to write when you are feeling angry too, so you can get the anger out. This can be your own secret journal that no one else reads, so you can write whatever you like in it.

No excuse

- You won't blame Asperger Syndrome for behaviours that you can control. If you really didn't forget something or you just feel like acting up, do not blame Asperger Syndrome.

Charts

- You can learn Social Stories™, e.g. 'What to do to catch a bus'.

- You can use your charts and timetables at home and school.

- You can draw up your own charts at home if you think you need help with getting ready for school in the morning.

- They will help you learn routine, then one day you won't need the charts anymore because you know them off by heart.

Changes

- A change might be that your class was going on an excursion to the zoo and you were very excited, but the weather was bad and your excursion was cancelled. This is disappointing and can make you sad or angry.

- If you understand that you can't stop changes, then you won't get so upset about them.

- When there is a change that you don't like, you can take a deep breath, and try to relax because you can't do anything about it.

- If you have to go somewhere new you can ask questions about that new place so you become familiar with it.

Happy

- You can try to be happy and not worry about lots of things.

- You can try to enjoy each day even when you don't feel like it.

- You can try not to worry about the future because you can enjoy today first.

- Being sad and negative can be a waste of your energy, it does not achieve anything.

Try

- If you find something hard to do or say, you can try not to get stressed but can ask for help,

e.g. if you are trying to solve a puzzle and it doesn't quite fit. You can even have a rest and go back to it a little later when you are feeling calmer. You can't always do well at everything, but if you try, you might just succeed!

Scales of Success

With all the help from yourself and from others around you, as you grow up your talents and personality traits will weigh heavier and your challenges will weigh less.

Label the left side of the weighing scales 'Talents' and the other 'Challenges'.

Write on the 'Talents' side of the scales all the things you are good at, and find easy to do.

On the 'Challenges' side, write the things you need help with.

Discover what happens…

Always remember:
Your Talents and Personality will always outweigh your Challenges.

You Are Very Special

An acrostic is a series of words where the first letters of each line spell out another word or phrase. Write an acrostic using your name, using special words about you.

For example, if your name is Sam:

S uper

A rtistic

M usician

Remember, everybody has a challenge of some kind,
It might be big or small,
They might need lots of help
Or none at all.
A disability might be if someone can't swim, can't read,
Needs help with maths or if they have a big mole on
their nose!
We're all special people in this world.
Nobody is perfect!
(Not even the Prime Minister or the President!)
Shhh!! Don't tell them I said that!

Visit Josie's website: www.booksbyjosie.com.au